IMAGES OF ENGLAND

COVENTRY TRANSPORT 1884–1940

IMAGES OF ENGLAND

COVENTRY TRANSPORT 1884–1940

ROGER BAILEY

TEMPUS

First published 2006

Tempus Publishing Limited
The Mill, Brimscombe Port,
Stroud, Gloucestershire, GL5 2QG
www.tempus-publishing.com

British Library Cataloguing in Publication Data.
A catalogue record for this book is available from the British Library.

ISBN 0 7524 3776 3

Typesetting and origination by Tempus Publishing Limited.
Printed in Great Britain.

Contents

Acknowledgements

Over the years there have been many people who have helped me, sometimes without even realising it. Special thanks to David McGrory, a true Coventry historian; Mike Lane for the use of his photographs; TN Lens for the use of many of the late A.J. Owens's photographs, who very generously made their views available and who provide a great service to the bus enthusiast.

Also to the memories of both Mr Whitehead, the son of the original General Manager, and Mr Stringer; both of whom I spent many hours talking with about old Coventry and who allowed their photographs to be copied for future use, which in both cases took many years to happen. Some of their photographs have been seen for sale in recent times, but the examples used here are from the originals and in some cases, glass negatives.

Thanks also to my fellow bus enthusiasts, amongst them – David Wyles, Timothy Boads, John Burton and Malcolm Curtis, for their help in making this possible. A number of original photographs have been used, where the original photographer is not known and the author would welcome further information on these.

I would like to dedicate this book to the crews who, over the many years, worked on the trams and buses in the city's own transport fleet. Especially my mum and dad, Maurine Bailey and Jim Bailey who both worked on the buses in Coventry from the 1950s to the 1980s.

Introduction

A number of books have been produced on transport in Coventry over the years, all now out of print, which seems a shame with so much interest in Coventry transport and with so many people now talking about the city's past. When Coventry lost its local transport system in 1974, for many it lost something big and important that played a vital part in people's lives in the twentieth century.

One of the main reasons for producing this book was to therefore give back some of that lost era using the many photographs and material available. A number of items featured have not been seen before, making this even more interesting. Today a lot of material is kept in archives and personal collections and so this is one way of showing a small part of this memorabilia to a wider audience, and not just the select few. Unlike others, this is not a purely technical book for the bus enthusiast and will therefore not cover all aspects of the vehicles. It is instead intended to be an enjoyable and nostalgic remembrance of a bygone age.

The first steam tramway started operating in 1884 from Coventry railway station to Bedworth, the proposed extension to Nuneaton having been withdrawn. The service operated for about four years before being suspended, and then continued again until 1893 when it was withdrawn. The line was then electrified and started operating again in December 1895 by the Coventry Electric Tramways Company, being quickly extended across the city over the next few years. In 1912 Coventry Corporation purchased the business and, after the First World War, set about improving the system by doubling the track and creating more extensions.

The first buses entered service in 1914 but their lives were short-lived as the chassis were commandeered for the war effort, and the bodies sold for further use. By 1919 new improved buses started appearing. Interestingly, they were mostly produced by the local company Maudslay, until the general manager T.R. Whitehead, retired in 1932 and his replacement Mr Fearnley took over. At this point the bus fleet changed overnight, and with a new manager came new ideas – Coventry very quickly showing to be a leading light in bus design, pushing trams quickly into the background. From that moment on nearly all deliveries were produced by Daimler – but for many an AEC engine was used.

Coventry was the first to try this combination, which it continued to order whenever possible for many years to come.

Probably the biggest step forward was the delivery in the late 1930s of the first two-axle double-deckers with an all-metal body for sixty passengers. In comparison to several years previous, this was a dramatic moment in the history of the corporation and in bus design in general. But in the years leading up to the Second World War, where this book finishes, the expanding engineering industry and growing population caused a big need to quickly increase the bus fleet.

one

Early
Transport

Until the late 1890s most local horse transport services were in actual fact railway feeders to local hotels such as the Kings Head, Craven Arms, Queens Hotel and the Wheatsheaf. For a limited time there was also a route from Broadgate to Bell Green. This photograph is the only view known of a local horse-bus service, run by a company called the 'Coventry Omnibus Company' around the turn of the century.

There are suggestions that there was once a stone tramway between Coventry and Nuneaton, dating back to the early 1800s, but little is known about it. It had been hoped to run a system from Coventry to Nuneaton towards the end of that century, but due to opposition, it never happened.

The steam tramway was never a large system unlike some other places, basically consisting of just the one route from Broadgate to Bedworth, starting in 1884 and only just managing to reach 1893 before it was abandoned. This is an example of the several engines and six trailers bought for the operation.

The Coventry Electric Tramways Company operated the trams from their first run in 1895, until being taken over by Coventry Corporation in 1912. The first four electric trams were numbered 1–4 and arrived in time for the launch. They had seats for forty passengers and were sometimes compared to horse-bus bodies, which were still operating in many parts of the country. This is one of those first four, pictured in 1896, with its rare Coventry Electric Tramways Limited fleet name, as used until about 1897.

Another of the first batch of four trams, this time with the later post-1912 Coventry Corporation Tramways fleet name. (*Whitehead*)

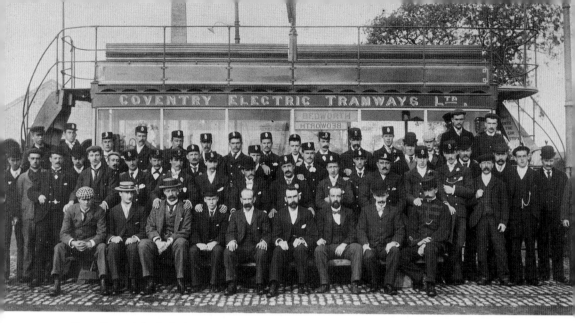

Six trailers originally built to operate on the steam system, were later converted to operate as electric trams. Numbers 5–8 were ready for the launch of the system in late 1895, and 9 and 10 the following year. This is believed to be one of those trailers, number unknown. With a group of employees in front, it has only just been made ready for service and could have been taken at the opening of the system. Note the early fleet name of Coventry Electric Tramways Ltd, which is rarely seen in photographs as it was only briefly used. Coventry Electric Tramways Company was more common. (Whitehead)

When the system was made electric, both trams and trailers were put into operation. The bodies of these trailers were later used to replace the bodies of the former steam trailers, this being the new tram 9 in Binley Road.

The first additional batch of electric trams were numbered 11–20 and arrived between 1897 and 1898 to seat a capacity of fifty-two. This posed photograph was taken in the very early days, with Ford Street on the right. *(Whitehead)*

Another tram from the same batch, number 18, which had clearly been in service a while. The picture was taken at the tram depot with a number of others in the fleet. *(Travel Lens)*

Again, a tram from the same batch, this time seen in Broadgate. Note the lack of decency boards on the top deck, discouragement for young ladies to travel on the upper level. Also notice the escape ladder to the right, a feature of many shots of Broadgate in the early days. This is another rare photograph as it shows the original number 20 which, along with number 19, passed to Norwich in 1905.

Batch 19–30 arrived in 1905, with the first two being replacements for two from the previous batch. They were second-hand from Wigan and could seat forty-six people. This is number 23 located in the tram depot, with replacement 19 in the background *(Travel Lens)*

A further tram from the same batch, number 28 is here seen at the terminus in Bedworth. They were easy to spot as a batch because they were the first to have only three windows on the bottom deck.

Batch numbered 31–36, had its bodies built by Milnes Voss, again with three windows each side. They arrived in 1907 and were capable of carrying fifty people seated. Again taken in the depot, this is number 34 with Alf Owen as driver. *(Travel Lens)*

Coventry
(OFFICIAL)
Electric Tram Time Table.

MAY—OCTOBER, 1902.

ASK FOR

Three Spires Brand

MALTED FOOD

FOR INFANTS.

Best substitute for Mother's milk.

FOR INVALIDS.

The most perfect and easily-digested Food.

To be obtained from all Chemists.

The front cover of a tram timetable from 1902.

TIME TABLE.

TRAMCARS.

Station to Broadgate.   Service No. 1 or 5.

Cars leave on the hour, 6, 12, 18, 24, 30, 36, 42, 48 and 54 mins. past the hour from 6.48 a.m.

WEEKDAYS. First car 5.52 a.m., 6.0, 6.6, 6.18, 6.24, 6.36, 6.43 a.m., then every 6 mins. until 11.6 p.m. Sats. 11.42 p.m.

SUNDAYS. First car 12.12, 12.24 p.m., then every 6 mins. until 11.6 p.m.

············

Broadgate to Station.   Service No. 1 or 5.

Cars leave on the hour, 6, 12, 18, 24, 30, 36, 42, 48 and 54 mins. past the hour from 6.42 a.m.

WEEKDAYS. First car 5.46 a.m., 6.0, 6.12, 6.18, 6.30, 6.42 a.m., then every 6 mins. until 11.0 p.m. Sats. 11.36 p.m.

SUNDAYS. First car 12.6, 12.18 p.m., then every 6 mins. until 11.0 p.m.

Broadgate to Earlsdon.   Service No. 7.

Cars leave on the hour, 12, 24, 36 and 48 mins. past the hour from 6.24 a.m.

WEEKDAYS. First car 6.24 a.m. then every 12 mins. until 11.0 p.m. Sats. 11.12 p.m.

SUNDAYS. First car 12.12 p.m. then every 12 mins. until 11.0 p.m.

On Saturdays cars run every six minutes from 5 p.m. to 9 p.m.

A page from a 1933 Coventry timetable, showing the level of service on the trams in the city.

An interesting photograph, believed to have been taken during the latter part of the First World War. It shows the General Manager, T.R. Whitehead, with all the female employees then working for the corporation to replace the men who had gone off to war. *(Whitehead)*

Another group, this time with a tram – showing the year as 1924 – and two recently delivered double-deck buses. The tram was being used to raise money for those who died during the First World War. The War Memorial Park along Kenilworth Road had opened in 1921.

A batch of five trams numbered 37–41 with bodies by Brush, were purchased in 1910 from Norwich where they had been new ten years previously. They were similar to trams 11–20 but had a larger capacity and were able to carry as many as sixty passengers seated. This is tram 38 in Broadgate in 1935.

A real oddity was tram 42, built in 1912–1913. Originally started by Coventry Electric Tramways, but on the change of ownership in 1912, was finished by Coventry Corporation Tramways. It had seats for fifty passengers. *(Whitehead)*

Left: Three trams delivered in 1913 were 43–45, with seats for forty-eight passengers and bodies built by Brush. This early shot of number 45 clearly shows the symbol used to indicate the route it was working on, plus a route number. The location is in Earlsdon at the terminus.

Below: A further photograph of the same batch taken in Bell Green and clearly showing the later destination configuration on tram 43. Also note the white lining which indicates that this was taken during the war, probably in 1940.

Opposite below: Tram 52 from the same batch, but with a different destination screen, is seen here in Broadgate.

Above: The batch numbered 46–53 was delivered over a three-year period starting in 1913, with Brush bodies and room for forty-eight people. These were the first to have roofs, though were otherwise similar to the previous delivery, having been ordered at the same time. The last of this batch was ordered as a replacement for a damaged tram. Pictured is tram 46 in Earlsdon. Notice the full destination display.

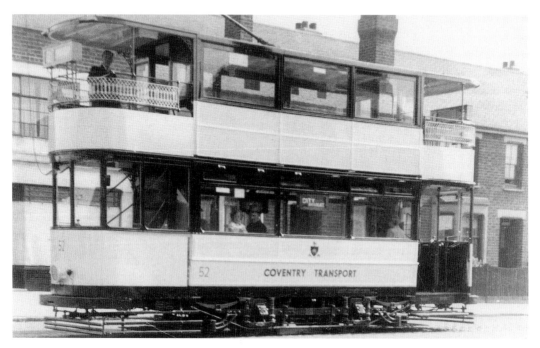

Another shot of tram 52, but this time painted in an all–cream livery, around May 1940. It would certainly stand out in the dark. Due to the destruction in November 1940 of the whole tram system, this tram would have only run in such condition for about six months.

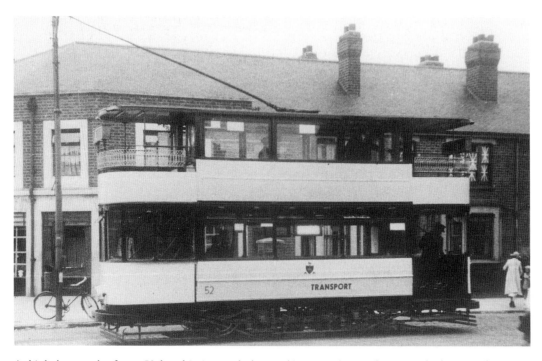

A third photograph of tram 52, but this time with the word 'Coventry' painted out. No doubt to confuse the enemy had we been invaded!

COVENTRY'S 5 THEATRES

SCALA
FAR GOSFORD STREET
'Phone 3429

GLOBE
PRIMROSE HILL STREET
'Phone 3813

RIALTO
RADFORD
'Phone 2112

REGAL
FOLESHILL ROAD
'Phone 8312

ASTORIA
ALBANY ROAD
'Phone 2056

CARLTON
STONEY STANTON ROAD
'Phone 8548

ALWAYS VISIT A " FIVE-STAR " THEATRE

NOW OPEN

THE RIALTO CASINO
Coventry's Dancing Rendezvous

A typical advertisement of the period, found in a 1937 timetable, publicising the various theatres of the city.

The next batch of trams, which arrived in 1921, were the first to be delivered after the Great War. Numbered 54–58, with bodies built by Brush and room for fifty seated passengers, they were similar in many ways to the previous batch. This shot, sold as a postcard, is of tram 55 in Bell Green.

Above: Another tram from the same batch, number 58, on Foleshill Road.

Opposite below: Another five trams, built by English Electric and similar in many ways to the previous batch, were bought in 1929 and numbered 64–68. This photograph shows tram 68 with the later fleet names and a white band indicating it was taken during the war before the system was destroyed. Parts of tram 68 were still visible in a garden in Allesley until 2000 when a few bits of the remains were rescued and have now been saved.

Above: Tram 61 was part of a batch of five trams bought in 1925, numbered 59–63 and built by Brush with seats for fifty-five people. This scene is in Broadgate, 1931, looking at the symbol still used to indicate the route. It was in 1933, after the arrival of the new General Manager, that new destination boxes replaced service number boxes and route symbols on all trams.

In 1931 the last trams were delivered for service in the city, numbered 69–73 and made by Brush with seats for fifty-five passengers. Seen as fast and steady, they were normally associated with the Stoke route. This is tram 71 coming round the corner from Vernon Street. It is worth noting that tram 71 has now been saved from a garden in Guildford. (Stringer)

Another tram from the same batch, number 72, is featured in Broadgate on a postcard. Note the bus in the background.

There was a proposal to look into the use of trolleybuses, and a double-decker was tried for a few days along Stoney Stanton Road, but it did not go any further.

A postcard of Smithford Street in 1928 shows how narrow many of the roads were in this mostly medieval city; this being the main reason why the track gauge was only 3ft 6in. Coventry during the War of the Roses was in all but name the medieval capital of England.

Another postcard of Broadgate taken in 1932 clearly shows the three tramlines in use. The bank in the background is still there, as is Hertford Street to the right.

The interior of Tram 32 which was found at Maxstoke, having once been used as a summer house. *(Bailey)*

When the Coventry Ring Road was being built, the original
tramlines were found still in the ground – this shot was taken at the
time in the late 1960s, near the old fire station. Recent excavations
during the making of Millennium Place surfaced them once more,
but it was decided to cover them up again for future discovery!
(Bailey)

ALTERATION OF

SERVI
Cars every 10 minutes, increasing to ev
All Services to cor

Commencing on SUNDAY, AUGUST 27th, 1933, the Tramw

From	To	Days	First Car	Frequency	Las
			a.m.		p.
Coventry Station	Bedworth ...	Sundays	10-5	10-25 a.m. then every 20 mins. until 12-5 p.m. ,, ,, 10 ,, ,,	1 (To F 1
		Weekdays	5-55	6-15 a.m. ,, ,, 20 ,, ,, 6-55 a.m. ,, ,, 10 ,, ,,	1 10-55 (To F 1
Broadgate ...	Windmill Road	Weekdays	5-40	6-0 a.m. ,, ,, 20 ,, ,, 7-0 a.m. ,, ,, 5 ,, ,, 9-30 a.m. ,, ,, 10 ,, ,, 12-0 noon ,, ,, 5 ,, ,, 2-30 p.m. ,, ,, 10 ,, ,, 5-0 p.m. ,, ,, 5 ,, ,, 7-0 p.m. ,, ,, 10 ,, ,, Fris. & Sats. every 5 mins. from noon	1
Coventry Station	Bell Green ...	Sundays	10-0	10-20 a.m. then every 20 mins. until 12-0 noon ,, ,, 10 ,, ,,	1 (To Stre
		Weekdays	6-0	6-40 a.m. ,, ,, 10 ,, ,,	1 (To Stre 11-1
Broadgate ...	Courthouse Green	Weekdays	6-5	6-45 a.m. ,, ,, 10 ,, ,, 7-15 a.m. ,, ,, 5 ,, ,, 9-30 a.m. ,, ,, 10 ,, ,, 11-55 a.m. ,, ,, 5 ,, ,, 2-30 p.m. ,, ,, 10 ,, ,, 4-55 p.m. ,, ,, 5 ,, ,, 7-5 p.m. ,, ,, 10 ,, ,, Fris. & Sats. every 5 mins. from noon	1
Earlsdon ...	Stoke ... via Paynes Lane	Sundays	10-4	10-24 a.m. then every 20 mins. until 12-4 p.m. ,, ,, 10 ,, ,,	1
		Weekdays	6-44	6-54 a.m. ,, ,, 10 ,, ,, (between 5-4 p.m. and 9-14 p.m. on Sats., every 5 mins.)	1 (11-
Broadgate ...	Kingsway ... via Ford Street	Sundays	10-2	10-22 a.m. then every 20 mins. until 12-2 p.m. ,, ,, 10 ,, ,,	1
		Weekdays	6-42	6-52 a.m. ,, ,, 10 ,, ,,	1 (11-2

Alterations to the tram routes.

ERVAL.

**ninutes at busy periods, on certain routes.
earlier on Sundays.**

vices on Sundays and Weekdays will be altered as follows:—

From	To	Days	First Car	Frequency	Last Car
			a.m.		p.m.
worth ...	Coventry Station	Sundays	10-5	10-25 a.m. then every 20 mins. until 12-5 p.m. ,, ,, 10 ,, ,,	10-35
		Weekdays	5-35	5-55 a.m. ,, ,, 20 ,, ,, 6-35 a.m. ,, ,, 10 ,, ,,	10-35 (11-5 Sats.)
dmill Road	Broadgate ...	Weekdays	5-50	6-10, 6-30, 6-50, 7-0 a.m. then every 5 mins. until 9-30 a.m. ,, ,, 10 ,, ,, 12-0 noon ,, ,, 5 ,, ,, 2-30 p.m. ,, ,, 10 ,, ,, 5-0 p.m. ,, ,, 5 ,, ,, 7-0 p.m. ,, ,, 10 ,, ,, Fris. & Sats. every 5 mins. from noon	10-50
Green ...	Coventry Station	Sundays	10-5	10-25 a.m. then every 20 mins. until 12-5 p.m. ,, ,, 10 ,, ,,	10-35
		Weekdays	5-35	6-25, 6-45 ,, ,, 10 ,, ,,	10-35 (10-45 Sats.)
rthouse Green	Broadgate ...	Weekdays	5-40	6-30, 6-50 ,, ,, 10 ,, ,, 7-10 a.m. ,, ,, 5 ,, ,, 9-30 a.m. ,, ,, 10 ,, ,, 12-0 noon ,, ,, 5 ,, ,, 2-30 p.m. ,, ,, 10 ,, ,, 5-0 p.m. ,, ,, 5 ,, ,, 7-0 p.m. ,, ,, 10 ,, ,, Fris. & Sats. every 5 mins. from noon	10-40 (10-55 Fris.) (and Sats.)
ke ... Paynes Lane	Earlsdon ...	Sundays	10-14	10-34 a.m. then every 20 mins. until 11-54 a.m. ,, ,, 10 ,, ,,	10-54
		Weekdays	6-14	6-34 a.m. ,, ,, 10 ,, ,, (between 5-4 p.m. and 9-14 p.m. on 2820 e.a Sats. every 5 mins.)	10-54
gsway ... Ford Street	Broadgate ...	Sundays	10-12	10-32 a.m. then every 20 mins. until 11-52 a.m. ,, ,, 10 ,, ,,	11-12
		Weekdays	6-52	7-2 a.m. ,, ,, 10 ,, ,,	11-12 (11-32 Sats.)

COVENTRY CORPORATION TRANSPORT.

DIAGRAM OF REGULAR TRAMWAYS AND BUS ROUTES, INDICATING
WORKS, AMUSEMENT HOUSES, PARKS, SPORTS' GROUNDS, ETC., ETC.

N.

BEDWORTH
.1.

• EXHALL COL.

KERESLEY
.6.

COVENTRY COLLIERY

LENTON'S LAN
.6.

ALDERMANS
GREEN.6.

HEN LANE
.3.

STADIUM

DOVEDALE

BROWNSHILL GREEN
.10 & 12.

FOLESHILL
PARK.
DUNLOP Wᴷˢ
HOLBROOK Bᴼˢ

BROOKVILLE
RILEY Wᴷˢ

FOLESHILL
.2 & 3.

BELL GREEN
5

COURTAULDS
Wᴷˢ

POOL L.
"TABB"
Wᴷˢ

HERBERTS
Wᴷˢ

CARLTON

RADFORD
.2.

FOLESHILL
PRINTING Wᴷˢ

MORRIS Wᴷˢ

ALLESLEY
.7 & 10.

CASHS Wᴷˢ

GRAND

BROAD Sᵀ
.6.

WALSGRAVE
6

COURTAULDS

BARKERS' BUTTS
LANE .5.

DAIMLER Wᴷˢ

STANDARD
Wᴷˢ

P. OF WALES
ROVER
Wᴷˢ

STOKE HEATH
.1

REDESDALE

BROAD LANE
.9.

RIALTO

GLENDOWER
AVENUE. 11.

MAUDSLAY
ROAD .1.

ALVIS
Wᴷˢ

RUGBY
Wᴷˢ

HIPPODROME

GLOBE

SINGER Wᴷˢ

TRIUMPH Wᴷˢ

DOG TRACK

CHAIR

ALEX.
BTH

CITY FOOTBALL GROUND

OPERA
HOUSE

PLAZA

GUDE

SCALA

GOSFORD Gᴺ

STOKE
.7 & 8.

GAUMONT

MORRIS

G.E.C.W

TILE HILL
8

HEARSALL
COMMON

STANDARD GAUGE & TOOL Cᴼ
WKS. EARLSDON
.7.

STIVICHALL
COMMON

BROADWAY

MAUDSLAY Wᴷˢ
STATION
.1 & 5.

MEMORIAL
PARK

HUMBER
HILLMAN Wᴷˢ

ARMSTRONG
SIDDELEY WKS.

WHITLEY
COMMON

STOKE
ALDERMOOR
.3.

BINLEY
.5.

GREEN LANE
2

ARMSTRONG
WHITWORTH
AERODROME.

'Buses shewn in Red.

Tramways shewn in Black.

A copy of the tram and bus routes still showing the Opera House, which dates it to the early 1930s.

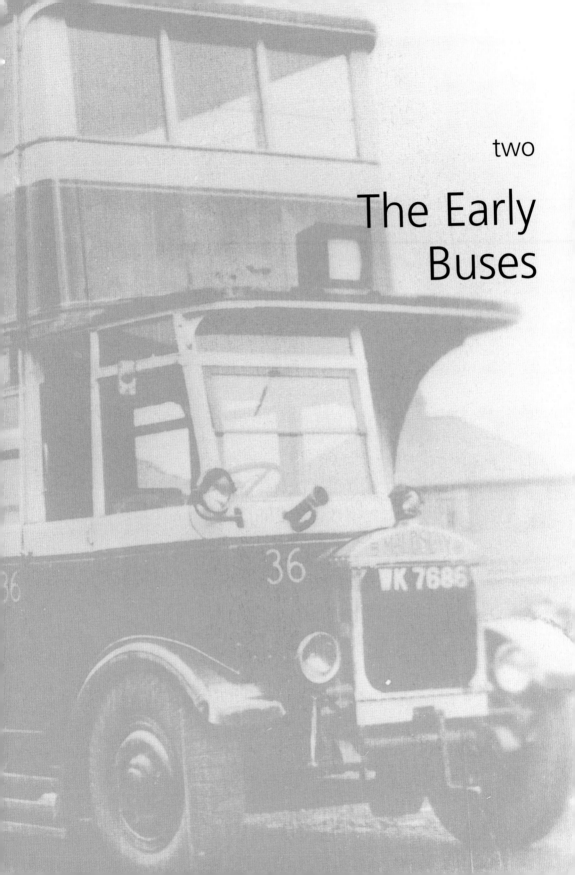

two

The Early
Buses

Above: A new chassis was launched by the Maudslay company in 1912 and known as the 3-tonner. Six of these were bought in 1914 for the first bus service in the city. They operated on a route from the Council House to Stoke Heath. This is the last of the batch, number 6, seen as new.

The AEC Y type was launched in the mid-1910s, and in 1919 Coventry bought seven with Hora bodies; fleet numbers 1–7. Towards the end of the decade some were fitted with pneumatic tyres; an unusual purchase for a city which had its own manufacturing facilities. This postcard features number 4.

Above: A further vehicle in the batch was number 7. These vehicles re-launched bus services in the city, including this one to Stoke Heath. *(Travel Lens)*

Opposite below: Number 6 seen later in service. These buses saw little use as they were all impressed by the War Office in the same year they were bought, and the bodies sold for service in Sheffield.

This postcard shows one of the first batches of Maudslay single-deck buses, with many of the crew who worked on them, plus members of the management.

The next batch was numbered 8–11. Number 9 can be seen here peeping out of the bus garage at Priestley's Bridge, with one of the AECs. By 1928 all were fitted with pneumatic types. This new delivery helped to expand bus services, including one to Foleshill Railway Station from the London road which was later extended. *(Whitehead)*

Maudslay later produced the 7-ton chassis for both lorry and bus use, known as the CP. The first one was bought by Coventry in 1923, carried fleet number 12 and came with a fifty-eight-seater Hickman body and a full-front cab. This photograph was taken when it was new. *(Whitehead)*

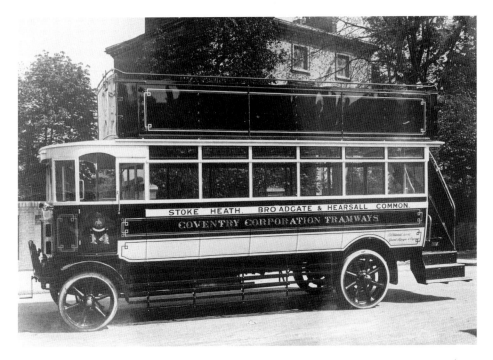

After the delivery of number 12 were a further four over the following two years. This is number 14, again seen as new. *(Whitehead)*

Outside the Council House, itself fairly new, are two buses geared up for a special occasion, but what is it? Of interest is the vehicle on the left with an emergency exit on the nearside. These are clearly of the batch of five vehicles numbered 12–16, either 15 or 16. Note also the vehicle behind from the 17–19 batch. *(Whitehead)*

In 1925, Maudslay introduced a low level frame version and the city was quick to show interest by buying three, with Hickman fifty-four-seat bodies, roofs for the first time and an open staircase. These were numbered 17–19 and the mark became known as the CPL, a low level frame variant. This is number 17 in service to Upper Stoke. *(Stringer)*

Another photograph of the same batch of three vehicles, this time showing a full side view outside the bus depot. *(Whitehead)*

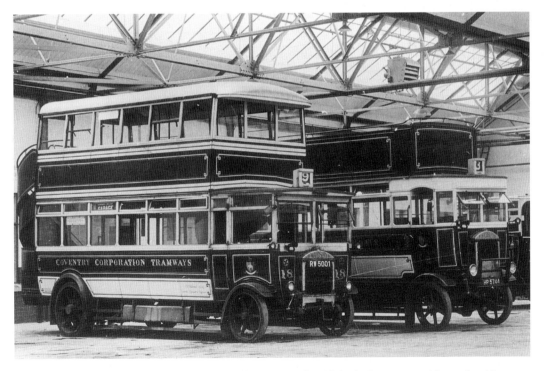

A further shot of the same batch of three, this time number 18 in the bus garage with number 12 standing next to it. *(Whitehead)*

A single-deck chassis was introduced in 1924 known as the ML, and between 1927 and 1929 a good number were purchased with Hickman twenty-six-seat dual entrance/exit bodies. These were numbered 20–35 and classified ML4/26. Being suitable for one man operation, this helped to expand the number of bus services running in the city, including one along Keresley Road, which was quickly extended to serve Keresley Village. This is number 28. *(Travel Lens/Whitehead?)*

Another shot of the same bus, number 28, but from the nearside, with the later 'City of Coventry' fleet name along the sides. Although built for one-man operation, they were also used with crews. *(Travel Lens)*

A postcard showing another single-deck bus from the same batch travelling over the recently built bridge in Lockhurst Lane. Note the double-deck bus in the background, one of the very first with a covered top.

A photograph of the workshops at Harnall Lane, probably about 1930. The man standing on the left is believed to be Tommy Parsons, the foreman at the time. *(Whitehead)*

By 1929 an improved version of the Maudslay double-decker appeared which became known as the CPL2. Four were bought with Vicker forty-eight-seat bodies, receiving fleet numbers 36–39. This is number 35 in the later livery. *(Travel Lens)*

In the late 1920s and early 1930s, the six-wheel double-deck bus became the must-have accessory for many operators around the country. The city went for it in a rather big way by ordering no less than seventeen that were delivered between 1929 and 1931. All were built by Maudslay and were the only such vehicles made by the company. This is the first, number 40, probably a prototype and came with a full front cab, unusual in those days. *(Stringer)*

The chassis of this batch were designated ML7 and all carried Brush bodies with seats for sixty in different styles. This is number 43, which entered service the following year. Note its location in the bus garage next to one of the single-deckers, numbered 34. *(Whitehead)*

Fleet number 51, part of a batch of six delivered in 1930 on learner duty. *(Travel Lens)*

FOR—CITY, SUBURBAN
or LONG-DISTANCE SERVICE

There's a **MAUDSLAY** to meet your Specific requirements. Omnibuses:— 30-66 Passenger Types. Coaches:— 26-36 Seats————and MAUDSLAYS are unrivalled for Economical Running and Low Maintenance Costs.

A COMPARISON OF CAPACITY.
One of Coventry Corporation's Fleet of MAUDSLAYS—a "Magna" rigid-frame 60-66 passenger type double-decker, snapped alongside a MAUDSLAY 32-seater "Mentor" long-distance saloon coach.

LOW-LEVEL SAFETY

THE MAUDSLAY MOTOR CO., LTD., COVENTRY.

London: 64/70 VAUXHALL BRIDGE ROAD, S.W.1

A rare advert for the Maudslay ML7 six-wheeler which appeared in a copy of The Commercial Motor in 1931. A fantastic period advert which really captures the era.

A rear view of one of the six-wheelers as delivered, and clearly showing the layout of the rear platform. This is number 56, the fleet numbers for all seventeen being 40, 41–46, 48–53, and 55–58. Delivered the same year Pool Meadow bus station was opened – 1931.

A rare view of one of the six-wheel Maudslays turning into Albany Road. The photograph was taken from the roof of the Butts College just after it opened. *(Stringer)*

It is surprising that, as Daimler was also a city-based manufacturer, they missed out on the early orders, but one vehicle that was hired and later bought was a CF which came onto the scene in the late 1920s. To match the other single-deck buses bought, it had a Brush twenty-six-seat body and carried fleet number 47. *(AJ Owen)*

The Dennis E series made its appearance in 1925 – the city bought one numbered 54 in 1930 with a bodies built by Brush to seat thirty-two, a company that supplied the undertaking for many years. This particular model was based on the EV, which indicated that it had a 6-cylinder Dennis engine.

The last three pure Maudslays bought were numbered 59–61 and were ML7s, but with only two-axles and Brush bodies seating fifty. Interestingly, of all the fleet delivered up to 1932, only these three would last through the Second World War, being withdrawn in 1945 and 1946. This is number 61 in Whoberley Avenue. *(Travel Lens)*

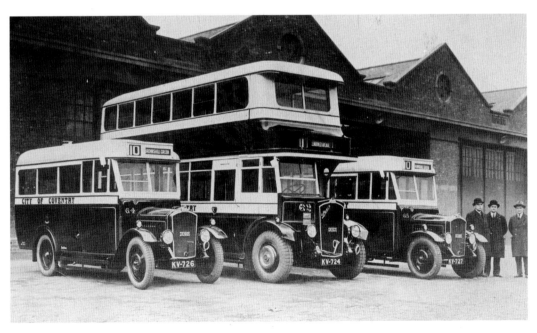

The Dennis Lance was introduced in 1931 and Coventry bought two, numbered 62–63, in the following year with Brush bodies. These were followed by two single-deck buses, again with Brush bodies, but with seats for only fourteen people, and initially used on a new service to Brownshill Green. Interestingly, the engines of these two buses were made by the Coventry firm White & Poppe.

An interior photograph of Harnall Lane bus garage showing one of the two Dennis Lance double-deckers, plus number 10, bought second-hand from the Coventry company Duckham, but withdrawn within a couple of years.

A terrific period shot taken in Broadgate in the late 1930s and sold as a postcard. Showing both a tram and one of the Maudslay six-wheelers.

These sorts of photographs are rare and could be first mistaken to be simple family views. In actual fact this shows the then general manager, T.R. Whitehead, with his family. Most of the fleet is lined up, including most of the six-wheel Maudslays. *(Whitehead)*

Another family shot with two Maudslay six-wheelers and one of the Dennis Lance double-deckers. Note the livery variation. *(Whitehead)*

A postcard showing the bottom of Bishop Street with the Old Grammar School to the right. Note the crossing of the two tramlines, and the bus and tram, the latter of which has white lines painted around the edge indicating that this was taken during the early part of the war.

One of the two fourteen-seaters based on a Dennis chassis, bus number 65, used initially for the 10 Brownshill Green service. Seen here in 1932 in Pool Meadow bus station just after it had been opened in 1931.

three

Buses of the 1930s

On the retirement of the General Manager, T.R. Whitehead, in 1933, his replacement, Ronald Fearnley, took over and quickly introduced a new era for the undertaking, including the ordering of a new fleet of buses. The first sixteen of these appeared in 1934 based

on the Daimler CP6 with petrol engines and Brush bodies for fifty people. Numbered 101–116, they were followed by further deliveries. This is the first which, after the trial of a demonstrator and in one swoop, saw the withdrawal of all vehicles built before 1926.

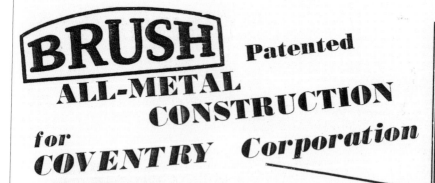

The following four pages feature advertisements from the era.

This one is for the first batch, plus a further delivery of numbers 120–122, as featured in The Transport World.

An advertisement linking Coventry's buses with the Commercial Motor Show at Olympia in 1935, as featured in The Commercial Motor. This was to promote the new MCW metal bodies. When the new buses were delivered, the livery was changed to maroon and cream.

30 YEARS DESIGNING AND BUILDING ROAD PASSENGER VEHICLES

As the result of nearly 30 years' experience in the designing and building of road passenger transport vehicles, the Daimler Company are to-day in the position to offer bus chassis which will meet all types of road conditions in an economical and efficient manner. The Daimler Fluid Flywheel Transmission alone places Daimler vehicles far in advance of other types, but apart from this consideration they incorporate many other unique features which enable Daimler to claim with complete confidence that they are offering the leading road passenger vehicles in the World to-day. A visit to Stand No. 82 at the Commercial Motor Transport Exhibition will enable you to inspect a fine range of Daimler vehicles and to meet technical representatives who will be happy to discuss your transport problems with you.

See the Daimler C.O.G.5 Chassis
ON STAND 82
COMMERCIAL MOTOR TRANSPORT
EXHIBITION — OLYMPIA
November 7th—16th.

DAIMLER COMPANY, LTD., COVENTRY.

A proud moment for Daimler and its association with Coventry Corporation, featuring the very first of the buses powered by AEC diesel engines, classified as COA6s. New destination boxes were introduced at the same time, becoming the new standard. These were side by side, a layout used in the fleet for decades to follow.

Fluid Flywheel Buses
again ordered by
COVENTRY
CORPORATION

Daimler Fluid Flywheel Buses are proving extremely popular in Coventry. The first 16 were ordered less than two years ago. A further order for six vehicles quickly followed and now we have pleasure in announcing a second repeat order for 20 double deckers of the C.O.A.6 type.

Company, Limited,
COVENTRY.

Part of the last batch with petrol engines, and an announcement for future deliveries having AEC diesel engines – a combination unique to the city before the Second World War.

The first three diesel buses were delivered in late 1934 and were numbered 117–119. Their classification was COA6, with AEC engines. They were also the first with all-metal bodies built by the Birmingham company Metropolitan Cammell Carriage and Wagon. *(MCCW)*

The second of the new buses in service, in Broadgate on its way to Green Lane.

Above: One of the first buses in service with an AEC Diesel engine, on its way to Radford via Broadgate.

Opposite below: Two hired buses, numbers 6 and 100, both double-deck Daimlers, were used in the city; number 6 being later bought. A Dennis GL was also bought second-hand and given fleet number 10, along with control of a works service, from W. Duckham. *(Travel Lens)*

Above: In 1935, further batches of the all-new Daimler buses had been delivered, including number 140, seen here in a line-up inside the bus depot at Harnall Lane. This was part of a batch which numbered 123–142. *(Travel Lens)*

There was still a need for smaller buses, especially on lightly used services. This is one of three Leyland Cubs with seats for twenty passengers bought for that purpose, number 144. *(Travel Lens)*

Trinity Street was opened in 1937, the same year as the first Owen and Owen, and when the New Hippodrome Theatre was revealed to the citizens of the city. This and Leyland Cub number 145 are all visible in this photograph, as is the Opera House. *(Travel Lens)*

This photograph is a little blurred, but shows one of the new double-deckers passing the New Coventry Theatre, with the old Opera House still standing in the background.

A group shot taken of the early buses, probably in the middle of the 1930s and clearly showing the rapid modernisation of the fleet.

Originally 127 but re-numbered to 427 in 1950 before being withdrawn in 1952. In the background is the building of the new Broadgate, this shot showing the area near Broadgate House.

Bus number 148, outside a camouflaged Coventry Theatre, probably in about 1946.

Bus number 146 at Burton Green – a Daimler COG5 which had a MCCW thirty-four-seat body – sold as a postcard like so many other bus scenes.

Another shot of bus 146, this time on service to Berkswell. The photograph was taken in the recently opened Pool Meadow bus station.

Commencing on SUNDAY, AUGUST 27th, 1933, th

From	To	First 'Bus	Frequency					Last 'E
		a.m.						p.m.
Stoke Heath	Maudslay Road	10-5	10-29 a.m. then every 24 mins. until 12-5 p.m. ,, ,, 12 ,, ,,					10-5
Green Lane...	Radford ...	10-6	10-30 a.m. ,, ,, 24 ,, ,, 12-6 p.m. ,, ,, 12 ,, ,,					11-6
Stoke Aldermoor	Hen Lane ...	10-0	10-24 a.m. ,, ,, 24 ,, ,, 12-0 noon ,, ,, 12 ,, ,,					11-0
Pool Meadow	Glendower Av.	10-0	10-30 a.m. ,, ,, 30 ,, ,, 12-0 noon ,, ,, 10 ,, ,,					11-0
Binley ...	Barkers' B. Lane	10-10	10-30 a.m. ,, ,, 20 ,, ,,					10-5
Alderman's G'rn	Keresley ...	10-25	11-25 a.m. ,, ,, 60 ,, ,,					9-25
Lenton's Lane	Keresley ...	9-55	10-55 a.m. ,, ,, 60 ,, ,,					9-55
Pool Meadow	Allesley ...	10-15	10-45 a.m. ,, ,, 30 ,, ,,					10-4
Pool Meadow	Tile Hill ...	10-0	10-30 a.m. ,, ,, 30 ,, ,, 4-0 p.m. ,, ,, 20 ,, ,,					11-0
Pool Meadow	Banner Lane (Broad Lane)	10-15	10-45 a.m. ,, ,, 30 ,, ,, 3-45 p.m.} 4-10 p.m.} ,, ,, 20 ,, ,,					10-5
Pool Meadow	Brownshill Gr'n	10-35	11-35 a.m. ,, ,, 60 ,, ,,					10-3

COVENTRY CORPORATION TRANSPORT.

Timetable for Sundays, showing updates starting in August 1933.

ON SUNDAYS.

ibus Services will commence and finish as under :—

From	To	First 'Bus	Frequency						Last 'Bus
		a.m.							p.m.
dslay Road	Stoke Heath	10-11	10-35 a.m. then every 24 mins. until	12-11 p.m. ,, ,, 12 ,, ,,					10-59
ford ...	Green Lane	10-6	10-30 a.m. ,, ,, 24 ,, ,,	12-6 p.m. ,, ,, 12 ,, ,,					10-54
Lane ...	Stoke Aldermoor	10-6	10-30 a.m. ,, ,, 24 ,, ,,	12-6 p.m. ,, ,, 12 ,, ,,					10-54
dower Av.	Pool Meadow	10-15	10-45 a.m. ,, ,, 30 ,, ,,	12-15 p.m. ,, ,, 10 ,, ,,					11-15
kers' B. Lane	Binley ...	10-0	10-20 a.m. ,, ,, 20 ,, ,,						11-0
esley ...	Alderman's Gr'n	10-25	11-25 a.m. ,, ,, 60 ,, ,,						9-25
esley ...	Lenton's Lane	10-55	11-55 a.m. ,, ,, 60 ,, ,,						9-55
esley ...	Pool Meadow	10-0	10-30 a.m. ,, ,, 30 ,, ,,						11-0
e Hill ...	Pool Meadow	10-23	10-53 a.m. ,, ,, 30 ,, ,,	4-23 p.m. ,, ,, 20 ,, ,,					11-23
ner Lane (Broad Lane)	Pool Meadow	10-8	10-38 a.m. ,, ,, 30 ,, ,,	4-8 p.m. 4-35 p.m. ,, ,, 20 ,, ,,					11-15
wnshill Gr'n	Pool Meadow	10-5	11-5 a.m. ,, ,, 60 ,, ,,						11-5

D A. FEARNLEY, A.M.I.A.E., M.Inst. ., General Manager and Engineer.

A photograph of the inside of Harnall Lane bus garage, taken in about 1938. An interesting selection of buses are on show, with one of the soon to be withdrawn Maudslay six-wheelers on the right (number 45), and number 6 in the middle, basically the demonstrator that started fleet modernisation.

A whole fleet of Daimler double-decker buses was delivered in the 1930s, all based on the type COA6. This shot taken in 1950 shows number 152 with its crew – one of whom is a David Jones – before leaving the bus depot.

Above: Bus number 153 at the terminus at the Red Lion in Walsgrave.

Opposite below: Another view of number 153, this time in Broadgate at night in the 1930s, before the city was to be reshaped by the Second World War.

Above: Again number 153, not long after delivery, and in service. *(Travel Lens)*

Bus number 170, another Daimler COA6, seen outside Holy Trinity Church just after the war.

Bus 171, seen in Jubilee Crescent, with the conductor showing off his new TIM ticket machine. *(Travel Lens)*

Further new single-deckers arrived in 1937 numbered 174–178, to be followed by others over the next three years. Two, 174 and 175, were painted in a reverse livery. This is the first just after delivery.

Another photograph of bus number 174 in service, in this case on the Outer Circle, which proved a very popular service, especially for sightseeing. The route was 30 miles long and was promoted as a tour of the city boundary.

Another shot of one of the new single-deck buses, this time bus 175. Again showing the conductor but with an older Bell Punch ticket machine. *(Travel Lens)*

Bus number 176, this time in the more standard livery, on its way to Burton Green but stopping for a photograph on Hearsall Common. *(Travel Lens)*

Bus number 182 with white markings, indicating a wartime shot. The bus behind is number 240 after a rebuild due to extensive damage during one of the bombing raids. The location is Corporation Street, in front of the building known for many years as the Gas Showrooms. *(Travel Lens)*

Similar bus 188 crossing Hearsall Common on its way to Tile Hill. Note the delivery van for Owen Owen following behind. *(Travel Lens)*

An interesting internal shot of Harnall Lane bus garage, probably taken in about 1938. It shows an interesting mix of Maudslays and more recently delivered single-deck Daimlers, including numbers 146, 174 and 176–178.

MOTOR OMNIBUSES.

Stoke Heath to Maudslay Hotel (via Council House).   Service No. 1.

'Buses leave at 5, 17, 29, 41 and 53 mins. past the hour from 6.53 a.m.

WEEKDAYS.   First 'bus 6.53 a.m., then every 12 mins. until 10.53 p.m. Sats. 11.5 p.m.

SUNDAYS.   First 'bus 12.17 p.m., then every 12 mins. until 10.53 p.m.

To Council House only.   Service No. 4.

WEEKDAYS.   Additional 'buses leave at 7.10, 7.27, 7.35, 7.39, 8.11, 8.35 and 8.47 a.m., 12.59, 1.23, 1.47, 2.11 and 5.25 p.m.

MONDAY TO THURSDAY. *'Buses run every 6 mins. from 5.29 p.m. to 8.17 p.m.*

FRIDAY.   *Every 6 mins. from 1.41 p.m. to 9.5 p.m.*

SATURDAY.   *Every 6 mins. from 12.17 p.m. to 4.53 p.m., then every 4 mins. until 11.5 p.m.*

SUNDAY.   *Every 6 mins. from 3.17 p.m. to 10.53 p.m.*

....

Council House to Maudslay Hotel.   Service No. 1.

'Buses leave at 6, 18, 30, 42 and 54 mins. past the hour from 6.54 a.m.

WEEKDAYS.   First 'bus 6.54 a.m., then every 12 mins. until 11.6 p.m. Sats. 11.18 p.m.
Additional 'buses : — Monday to Friday at 12.12, 1.0 and 5.40 p.m. to Hearsall Common.

SUNDAYS.   First 'bus 12.6 p.m., then every 12 mins. until 11.6 p.m.

A 1933 timetable showing frequency of services 1 and 4.

TO AND FROM HUMBER WORKS.

TO Humber.   FROM Humber.

LEAVE :—	MONDAY TO SATURDAY.	LEAVE :—
Coventry Station ...	7.42 a.m.	At 5.30 p.m., 6.0 p.m.
Do.	7.50 a.m.	Thurs., 12 noon Sats.

LEAVE :—	MONDAY TO FRIDAY.	LEAVE :—
Jeff. Wood's Cross	1.45 p.m.	
Vine Street	—	At 1.0 p.m.
London Road ...	—	

Fares to Humber Works from :—

Jeffrey Wood's Cross, 3d.; Stratford Street, Vine Street or Coventry Station, 2d.; London Road, 1½d.; Ball Hotel or Gosford Green, 1d.

....

TO AND FROM LONDON ROAD (PARKSIDE).

(For Armstrong Siddeley and Maudslay Works).

TO London Road.   FROM London Road.

LEAVE :—	MONDAY TO SATURDAY.	LEAVE :—
Stoke Heath ...	5.45 a.m.	At 6.0 a.m., 5.30 p.m. Thurs. 6.0 p.m. (Sats. 6 a.m. only).
Hen Lane	7.25 a.m.	
Do.	7.33 a.m.	At 5.35 p.m. Thurs. 6.5
Holbrook Lane ...	7.18 a.m.	p.m. 12 noon Sats.
Do.	7.22 a.m.	At 5.50 p.m. Mon. to
Do.	7.50 a.m.	Wed. only.
Do.	8.0 a.m.	

A 1933 timetable showing some of the special services to and from factories in the city.

A period trade advert from the magazine *Commercial Motor* in 1937 showing bus number 162
helping to promote the Brush body it carries.

Sixth Repeat Order —
Received from COVENTRY CORPORATION

for

BRUSH

Patented

All Metal
BUS BODIES

demonstrates conclusively the satisfaction given in service.

BRUSH Passenger Coachwork has been selected for quality by many Transport Undertakings and Operating Companies.

For Coachwork of Composite and Patented All Metal Construction.

Send your enquiries to:

BRUSH
COACHWORK LIMITED
LOUGHBOROUGH, ENGLAND

*A Book
to set you
thinking*

It will not appeal to those who accept excessive vehicle deadweight as a foregone "conclusion" of increased earning capacity. It describes in detail an entirely new principle in construction already proved in the case of goods vehicles and which can be applied "with profit" to Passenger Vehicle design . . . . it represents the most effective onslaught ever made on unprofitable deadweight. May we send you a copy?

REYNOLDS

TUBES, RODS, SECTIONS, SHEET & STRIP IN HIGH STRENGTH ALUMINIUM ALLOYS.

REYNOLDS TUBE COMPANY LTD.   REYNOLDS ROLLING MILLS LIMITED.
TYSELEY, BIRMINGHAM, 11

A second advert which appeared in *Bus & Coach* in 1939, featuring bus 203 which featured at the Commercial Motor Show in 1937 in London.

Bus number 197, parked in Trinity Street with construction still going on in the background. You can see the workmen's hut behind the bus and the original buildings in the background. The building which is now Wetherspoons had yet to be built.

Daimler double-decker number 199 seen with its new Roe body, as fitted in 1949. It was withdrawn in 1958 after 20 years in service, though gave another 3 years with a second operator.

A standard bus in the fleet but in reverse livery, this is the famous bus 205, delivered in 1938 the same year as the two single-deckers also painted in reverse livery. *(Travel Lens)*

Bus number 208, not long after delivery, on service in Baginton. The batch was numbered 206–211 and was based on the Daimler COG5 chassis, with Park Royal bodies. Further deliveries were numbered 242–244. Note the new TIM ticket machine.

The famous bus 205, as featured in yet another advertisement for Brush who made the body. This appeared in *Commercial Motor* in 1939.

Bus number 218 in the later livery for these vehicles, on service 20 in Bedworth waiting for the return journey.

Another from the same batch, number 220, delivered in 1939 and pictured outside the soon to be finished building which is today Wetherspoons. *(Travel Lens)*

Taken before entering service, bus 221 with the then standard fifty-six-seat Metro-Cammell body.

Bus number 222 from the same batch but in the later livery and seen in Allesley Village.

A typical Daimler COA6. This vehicle carried a Massey fifty-six-seat body and was the only one to do so at the time. The location is Pool Meadow originally opened in 1931, but the livery shows this to be a post-war shot. Note the one-person air-raid shelter next to the bus.

Bus 228 in post-war Broadgate showing the temporary shops in the background. This was the last but one bus with a body for fifty-six passengers, as those that followed had a larger capacity.

J. W. COURTENAY LTD

Advertising Contractors and Agents

Have Given

SPECIALISED & DEPENDABLE SERVICE TO THE PRINCIPAL TRANSPORT UNDERTAKINGS THROUGHOUT THE UNITED KINGDOM FOR OVER 70 YEARS

HIGHEST RENTALS OFFERED FOR SOLE ADVERTISING RIGHTS

HEAD OFFICE

AMBERLEY HOUSE, NORFOLK STREET, LONDON, W.C.2

TELEPHONE : TEMPLE BAR 7630   TELEGRAMS : COURTOWN, ESTRAND, LONDON

TRANSPORT WORLD

A rather unusual advertisement for the people who themselves advertised on Coventry buses. Featured in the magazine *Transport World*, the company clearly felt it was good to promote its partnership with the City of Coventry.

WORKPEOPLE'S SPECIAL SERVICES.
BUSES.
TO AND FROM WHITLEY AERODROME.

	TO WHITLEY					FROM WHITLEY					
	Mon to Sat.	Mon to Sat.	Mon to Fri.	Mon to Fri.	Sat. only	Mon & Fri.	Mon Tue. Wed Fri.	Th. only	Mon to Fri.	Tue. Wed Th.	Mon to Fri.
	A.M.	A.M.	P.M.	A.M.	noon	P.M.	P.M.	P.M.	P.M.	P.M.	P.M.
Stoke Heath	7 35	....	....	....	12 0	....	5 0	5 30	....	7 0	8 0
Broadgate	7 42	....	7 40	....	12 0	....	....	....	7 0	7 0	....
Coventry Station	7 45	....	....	....	12 0	....	5 0	5 30	....	7 0	....
Rialto	7 40	....	....	....	12 0	....	5 0	5 30	....	....	....
Gosford Green	7 45	7 50	....	8 0	12 0	....	5 0	5 30	....	7 0	8 0
Council House	7 43	7 49	7 41	8 0	12 0 & 1220	....	5 0	5 0 & 530	7 0	7 0	8 0
London Road	7 45	7 50	7 45	8 5	12 0 & 1220	....	5 0	5 0 & 530	7 0	7 0	8 0
Pool Meadow	7 43	....	....	....	....	....	....	....	....	....	....
Engleton Road	7 28	....	7 27	....	12 0	....	....	....	7 0	....	....
Wyken	7 37	....	....	....	12 0	5 0	....	....	7 0	....	....

Fares to Whitley Aerodrome from :—

Rialto or Stoke Heath, 4½d. ; Hastings Road, Barras Lane Garage or Pool Meadow,
4d.; Gosford Green, Council House, Broadgate, Coventry Station, London Road
or Stoneleigh Terrace, 3d.; Railway Bridge, Whitley Wharf, 2d.; Howes Lane, 1d.
For buses to Baginton Airport see Service No. 13, pages 53 and 54.
These Fares apply only to Special Works' Buses running direct between above points.

TO AND FROM G.E.C. WORKS (Stoke).

	TO G.E.C. WORKS.			FROM G.E.C. WORKS.				
	Monday to Saturday			Monday to Friday			Mon to Thu.	Saturday
	A.M.	A.M.	P.M.	N'N	P.M.	P.M.	P.M.	N'N
Hen Lane Corner	6 58	7 0	....	....	5 0	6 0	7 30	12 0
Jackson Road	6 58	....	....	....	5 0	6 0	7 30	12 0
Pridmore Road	7 0	....	....	....	5 0	6 0	7 30	12 0
Wright Street	7 10	7 12	....	....	5 0	6 0	7 30	12 0
Jeff. Wood's Cross	7 17	....	1245	12 0	5 0	6 0	7 30	12 0
St. George's Road	....	....	1250	12 0	....	....	....	....
Lenton's Lane	6 55	....	....	....	....	....	....	....
Walsgrave	7 5	....	1245	12 0	5 0	6 0	....	12 0
Wyken Pippin	7 10	7 15	1248	12 0	5 0	6 0	....	12 0
Beech Tree Avenue	6 55	....	....	....	5 0	....	....	12 0
Perkins Street	7 7	7 10	....	....	5 0	....	....	12 0

Fares to G.E.C. Works from :—

Lenton's Lane, Hen Lane or Beech Tree Avenue, 5½d. ; Letter Box, Lenton's
Lane, Holbrook Lane or Co-op Sports Ground, 4½d.; Shilton Lane or
Queensland Avenue, 4d.; Pridmore Road, 3½d.; Potters Green, Walsgrave or
Barras Lane, 3d.; Jeffrey Wood's Cross or Perkins Street, 2½d.; Bramble Street,
2d.; Junction of Walsgrave Road with Clay Lane, Wyken Grange, St. George's
Road, 1½d. ; Arterial Road, 2d. ; Burns' Road, 1d.
These Fares apply only to Special Works' Buses running direct between above points.
For times of buses to and from Barkers Butts Lane, see Service No. 5

A page from the 1937 timetable listing the various works services to the Whitley Aerodrome and GEC.

Left: An exterior shot of the first sixty-seater bus – number 230 – with an all-metal Brush body, delivered for service in the city and part of the batch 230–233. They were Daimler COG5s, the first of many, and seen here in Keresley. *(Travel Lens)*

Below: Not long after delivery and with white lining indicating the war period, this is bus number 231 from the same initial batch of sixty-seaters. Behind is Cheylesmore still being constructed and to the right you can just see the Cheylesmore Public House, recently demolished. *(Travel Lens)*

Above: An interior shot of the downstairs of one of the buses delivered in 1939, showing some of the twenty-nine seats that would have been on the lower level. With an additional thirty-one seats upstairs, it had a total capacity of 60 – the first of many of this size.

Below: Bus number 235 seen outside the original Herbert Art Gallery & Museum, next to the Council House. Today Browns stands on the site.

Above: The front cover of a 1937 timetable, which at that time would still feature both the bus and tram services in the city.

Opposite below: The lone Daimler with an AEC engine (COA6) delivered in 1940 was number 246, here seen after the war just outside Holy Trinity Church with Timothy White's Chemist in the background, a famous landmark in its day.

Above: Number 239 when new, part of the batch numbered 238–241, all being of the Daimler COG5 type with Brush sixty-seat bodies.

Above: The first of the last batch delivered in 1940, was number 247, all being of the COG5 type with bodies by Brush. It is here seen in Pool Meadow bus station after the war. Unusually, it still carries its metal strip around both destination boxes, an indication in the early days that it was a sixty-seater.

Midland Red operated services into the city from a variety of places. To help the company, a bus garage to house a small number of vehicles was built in Sandy Lane, opening in 1921 and closing a couple of years later when better facilities were made available in nearby towns. This is a SOS REDD built in 1933 with a Brush fifty-four-seat body. HA 8038 is on a stand in Pool Meadow bus station, on the famous Coventry to Birmingham 159 route, nowadays is known as Travel West Midlands 900.

Above: HA9459–SOS ON Short thirty-eight-seat body built in 1934. Along the new Corporation Street.

Opposite below: In post-war Broadgate with the temporary shops in the background, is number 256.

SOS IM6 with Short thirty-four-seat body built in 1933 – HA 8323. Note the fire station behind, then in use it has now been converted into a restaurant.

HA 9051–SOS LRR Short thirty-seat coach body built in 1933. It was converted into a bus in 1941 as a prototype of its class.